PREPARE NOW
for the
Temple

An Essential Guide for Young Adult Sisters

Dec 2007

Tiffani:

Words are never enough to express feelings or thoughts. I always struggle with it! Since the first day I met you I have been impressed, and have admired you. I am grateful for the short quality amount of time I was allowed to work with you, and that I got to know you better!

You are embarking on a grand adventure, and I truly wish you the best. This is a fantastic quick read, that will help you prepare.

All my love, Monica Jones

I just read it here in the store within 20 minutes! I love it! :)

PREPARE NOW *for the*

Temple

An Essential Guide for Young Adult Sisters

BRITTANY MANGUS

CFI
Springville, Utah

ISBN 13: 978-1-59955-052-7

Published by CFI, an imprint of Cedar Fort, Inc., 2373 W. 700 S., Springville, UT, 84663
Distributed by Cedar Fort, Inc. www.cedarfort.com

LIBRARY OF CONGRESS CATALOGING-IN-PUBLICATION DATA

Mangus, Brittany, 1979-
Prepare now for the temple / Brittany Mangus.
    p. cm.
Includes bibliographical references.
ISBN 978-1-59955-052-7 (alk. paper)
1. Mormon temples. 2. Temple endowments (Mormon Church) 3. Mormon women. 4. Marriage—Religious aspects—Mormon Church. I. Title.

BX8643.T4M36 2007
246'.9589332—dc22

2007013744

Cover design by Nicole Williams
Cover design © 2007 by Lyle Mortimer
Edited and typeset by Kimiko M. Hammari

Printed in the United States of America

10 9 8 7 6 5 4 3 2 1

Printed on acid-free paper

*And many people shall go and say,
Come ye, and let us go to the mountain of the
Lord . . . and he will teach us of his ways,
and we will walk in his paths. . . .
Come ye, and let us walk in the light of the Lord.*

—Isaiah 2:3, 5

For Que

Contents

Introduction

Thank you for being interested in preparing yourself to go to the temple. This book is designed for girls who are old enough to be engaged or preparing for a mission and young enough to be a new high school graduate. (I tailored this book for girls because, well, I'm a girl, and I wanted to mention subjects like the Young Women organization, temple weddings, wedding dresses, temple garments, and the clothing you choose to wear over them. I assume boys don't want to read about those subjects.) I hope that more girls who have just graduated from high school will begin to earnestly prepare for the temple so that they will not have to do a crash course on temple preparation when they find themselves engaged or preparing for a mission.

As a young girl raised in the Church, I was always fascinated by the temple. For me, it was more than a castle to get married in; it was a place to be closer to Heavenly Father and the Savior. It was "a house of learning" and "a house of God" (D&C 88:119). Of course, I didn't always understand what the temple was for or what went on there, but shortly after high school, I made a conscious effort to make sure I was thoroughly prepared to enter the

Lord's house. When I did go to the temple for the first time, I felt at peace and I enjoyed my experience. I want everyone who goes to the temple to feel the same way.

I am not claiming to be a gospel scholar or someone with all the answers. (I am still learning myself.) But this book can help you get started. I like to refer to it as "an appetizer in the buffet of temple knowledge." I hope you will read this book and decide you want to know more about temple worship. I hope this book shows you that learning about deep, doctrinal subjects like gospel symbolism can enrich your life and your future marriage and show you that learning more about these subjects is easy. This book will teach you the basics of what to expect the first time you attend the house of the Lord. But if you want to know what the *temple* can teach you, you'll need to return to the temple often and pray about your experiences there.

CHAPTER 1

How Do I Prepare
for the Temple ?

Preparing for the temple takes time

I'll be honest. I had no idea how to actually prepare for the temple. When I decided to make a sincere effort to do so, I quickly discovered it wouldn't be an overnight process. Preparing for the temple takes time. I think that is one of the reasons the Church asks adult converts to wait at least one year from their baptismal date before entering the temple.

Of course, the ideal situation is for young women who have been brought up in the Church to be constantly preparing for the temple. You can make a serious effort to prepare yourself to receive the temple ordinances even if you don't have a marriage prospect or don't plan to serve a mission. In my opinion, that is the best scenario to prepare because you're not under a deadline.

If you have been asking people how to prepare for the temple, you have probably been frustrated by their answers—I was. The answer I most commonly received was "read your scriptures and pray." I often thought, *Which passages of scripture should I read?* and *What exactly do I pray about?* While reading scriptures and seeking knowledge through prayer are excellent things to do, I have compiled a more precise list of things. (I have even listed specific scriptures for you later on in this book.) If you've been a member of the Church for more than a few years, you will have completed or participated in most of the following:

Ways to Prepare for the Temple

- Obtain Young Women Recognition Award.

- Graduate from Seminary.

- Choose friends (both male and female) who have the same goal of going to the temple.

- Read church magazines like the *New Era*, *Ensign*, and *Liahona*.

- Choose to only date temple-worthy young men.

- Receive your patriarchal blessing.

- Gain and feed a strong testimony.

- Obey the commandments and repent when necessary.

- Only wear modest clothing that could be worn with temple garments.

- Attend a temple preparation class.

- Attend college-level Institute classes, if available.

- Attend church regularly and study specific scriptures.

- Pray and meditate often.

- Read nonfiction, doctrine-related books.

All these things will help make you spiritually strong. I hope to steer you toward the last three points: careful prayer and reading the scriptures and doctrine-related books. Even if you don't receive your Young Women medallion or attend Seminary or Institute classes, you can still gain considerable knowledge about the gospel and prepare for the temple by studying on your own and praying about the things you learn. (I'm assuming you already have a testimony.)

A good way to begin is to read the specific scriptures that mention the temple or that directly correlate with temple ceremonies. Another good idea is to take a temple preparation class, which is generally available to members of the Church everywhere. Temple preparation classes are usually taught by a member from your ward, branch, or stake. However, temple preparation classes and this book are meant as supplements to your personal temple preparation studies. Neither is meant to be a crash course. (That's why it is good to always be preparing for the temple.)

Some young women are under the false impression that obtaining gospel knowledge is the sole responsibility of their future husband. If you want to have a deeper gospel understanding opened unto you while you're at the temple, you have to be willing to do some of the legwork yourself. Don't be afraid to read books about the gospel. However, not just any LDS book will do. Being able to say you've read the entire *The Work and the Glory* series by Gerald Lund may give you bragging rights, but it doesn't count as gospel doctrine study.

Why do I have to prepare, and what am I preparing for? Can't I just show up?

Just showing up to the temple unprepared is like showing up to go hiking in high heels and a skirt. Many outdoor enthusiasts become lost and trapped in the mountains every year because they head out into the wilderness unprepared. If they had only brought enough food or water or worn the correct clothing or shoes, their disaster could have been avoided. Experienced hikers know how to prepare. Just like hikers, temple-goers need to understand where they're going.

The temple is a symbol of our faith and of heaven itself. If people are confused about why they need to prepare, they most likely don't understand what the temple ceremonies are or even why they're going there in the first place.

Worthiness + Knowledge = Preparedness

As you are well aware, being worthy plays a large role in being prepared for the temple. However, it is not the only requirement. Below I have listed a few things you must do to remain worthy to worship in the temple and the knowledge you must have in order to be well prepared to worship there. One column without the other does not constitute temple preparedness—they must both be satisfied.

Worthiness	Knowledge
• Be chaste. • Obey the Word of Wisdom. • Attend all church meetings. • Pay tithing. • Be honest. • Do not affiliate with apostate groups or ideals.	• Have a testimony of Jesus Christ, prophets, modern revelation, the Book of Mormon, Joseph Smith, and the truthfulness of the gospel. • Know why you are attending the temple. • Know the purpose of the ceremonies.

A testimony is essential for temple worship. (A testimony is not *hope* but *knowledge* you have obtained through the Spirit of God.) Knowing why you are attending the temple and knowing the purpose of the ceremonies go hand-in-hand, and learning one will teach you about the other.

Many people attend the temple armed only with their worthiness and testimonies. They do not understand why they are there or what the temple ceremonies are. Some people come away content with their first visit to the temple, but some do not. In *House of Glory*, S. Michael Wilcox explains that his first temple experience left him "bewildered and a little frightened," but that happened only because he did not understand "the manner in which the Lord teaches his children in his house." He said, "Had I understood, my anxiety and confusion would have disappeared, even though my comprehension level might have remained the same."[1]

The good news

Not all doctrine-related books are boring or difficult to understand, nor were they all written for grandpas. At the end of this book (in a section titled "Further Light and Knowledge"), I have listed some books, magazines, specific scripture references, articles, and talks on tape or CD to get you started. You can even watch DVDs (from either an LDS-themed bookstore or from the Church Distribution Center) that deal specifically with the temple.

Prioritize

If you are (or have witnessed someone) getting ready to leave on a mission or planning a wedding, you know it takes a lot of time and preparation. The chart on page 6 lists only a few of the things that are needed, but you can get the idea.

Things I Need to Do Before I Enter the MTC	Things I Need to Do Before I Get Married
1. Buy new scriptures.	1. Find a dress.
2. Buy missionary clothing.	2. Reserve the temple and the reception center.
3. Get a passport.	3. Make sure all the bridesmaids have matching dresses and accessories.
4. Get a physical and the necessary shots.	
5. Prepare sacrament meeting talk.	4. Obtain the marriage license.
6. Have missionary portrait taken.	5. Address and mail the invitations.
7. Receive my endowment.	6. Order the wedding cake.
8. Pack for the MTC.	7. Buy presents for the bridesmaids.
9. Get all my friends' addresses so we can keep in touch.	8. Pick up my dress from the seamstress.
10. Choose a scripture for my missionary plaque.	9. Have my bridal portrait taken.
11. Research the area that my mission is in.	10. Receive my endowment.
	11. Attend the wedding dinner.
	12. Pack my bags for the honeymoon.

In the hectic atmosphere of planning either of these events, preparing to attend the temple and even attending the temple tends to get put on a to-do list, as if attending the temple for the first time is just something else you need to do so you can get married or leave on your mission. Avoid this at all costs. Wouldn't it be great if you were already prepared for the temple?

Preparation to attend the temple is more important than any other preparations you have to make. I think that most LDS brides make little effort to prepare themselves to enter the house of the Lord because they don't do it prior to being engaged, and then they're too busy trying to get everything else done. I hope the advice in this book will help you avoid that.

Obedience is the first law of heaven

A major part of being prepared for the temple is being obedient to the commandments. Merely "being a good person" is not enough. The Lord said, "If ye love me, keep my commandments" (John 14:15). Joseph Smith said, "Whatever God requires is right, no matter what it is, although we may not see the reason thereof till long after the events transpire."[2]

The principle of obedience has been essential since the beginning. After Adam and Eve were expelled from the Garden of Eden, an angel came to Adam and asked him why he was offering sacrifices. Adam said, "I know not, save the Lord commanded me." Then the angel explained to him that "this thing is a similitude of the sacrifice of the Only Begotten of the Father, which is full of grace and truth. Wherefore, thou shalt doest in the name of the Son, and thou shalt repent and call upon God in the name of the Son forevermore" (Moses 5:5–8). Even though Adam did not understand why he was supposed to offer sacrifices, he did it because he was commanded to.

No unclean thing

As you are probably already aware, in order to attend the temple, you will need a recommend. This requires you to attend personal interviews with your bishop and stake president. Elder Richard G. Scott said that "personal worthiness is an essential requirement to enjoy the blessings of the temple. *Anyone foolish enough to enter the temple unworthily will receive condemnation.*"[3] I don't know about you, but receiving condemnation is the last thing I want. The Lord said, "No unclean thing shall be permitted to come unto [my] house" (D&C 109:20). Although repentance is possible, it is easier to avoid the mistake in the first place.

No one is immune to temptation. Stay away from situations that can lead to temptation. These situations mostly stem from being alone with your fiancé. A good rule of thumb is to avoid situations like lying down together (even on a couch), getting under a blanket together, being in his or your bedroom together, staying up too late, vacationing together alone, or sharing hotel rooms.

If anything questionable has taken place, please talk it over with your bishop. The scriptures tell us, "If we confess our sins, [the Lord] is faithful and just to forgive us our sins, and to cleanse us from all unrighteousness" (1 John 1:9). The Lord said, "Though your sins be as scarlet, they shall be as white as snow; though they be red like crimson, they shall be as wool" (Isaiah 1:18). We wear white clothing in the temple to symbolize purity and worthiness to be in the house of the Lord. No one who attends the temple is perfect, but members are still deemed worthy by their bishops if they properly take care of any past indiscretions and continually strive to keep the commandments.

Notes
1. Wilcox, *House of Glory*, 11.
2. *Teachings of the Prophet Joseph Smith*, 201, 203.
3. Scott, *Ensign*; emphasis added.

CHAPTER 2

Why Receive Your Own *Endowment?*

Why are you choosing to receive your endowment?

If you said "because I'm going on a mission" or "because I'm getting married in the temple," you might want to reconsider your answer. Those are *occasions* that prompt people to receive their endowment, but they are not the *reason*. A better answer would be "so I can learn who I am, where I came from, where I can go after this life, and how to get there." And certainly one could say "so I can make further covenants with God." The word *endowment* means "gift," and the endowment's purpose is to arm you with knowledge. Likewise, the endowment gives you power. In Doctrine and Covenants 109:22, we can read the words Joseph Smith used in the Kirtland Temple dedication. He mentions "that thy servants may go forth from this house armed with thy power, and that thy name may be upon them, and thy glory be round about them, and thine angels have charge over them." In short, the endowment is literally a "gift of knowledge and power."

What is the temple endowment?

Before I received my own endowment, I read (and continue to read) extensively on the subject. It is interesting to note that of all the books I have read, I learned the most about the endowment from this 1853 quote from Brigham Young: "Your endowment is, to receive all those ordinances in the house of the Lord, which are necessary for you, after you have departed this life, to enable you to walk back to the presence of the Father, passing the angels who stand as sentinels, being enabled to give them the key words, the signs and tokens, pertaining to the Holy Priesthood, and gain your eternal exaltation in spite of earth and hell."[1]

Notice Brother Brigham didn't talk about participating in the endowment as purely a precursor to being sealed or going on a mission. As I have stated before, that is not the purpose of the endowment. As Brigham Young said, it is teaching you (amongst other things) how to get back to the presence of Heavenly Father.

Foster a humble attitude

The early Saints of the Church understood the value of the temple ceremonies. "Joseph Smith realized that his time on earth was short, so while the [Nauvoo] temple was still under construction, he began giving the endowment to selected faithful followers in the upstairs room of his red brick store."[2]

On 10 December 1845 (eighteen months after Joseph Smith was killed), the first endowment ceremonies were conducted inside the Nauvoo temple. Before they were driven from the city, 5,615 Saints received their endowments.[3] "The Saints were so anxious to receive this sacred ordinance that Brigham Young, Heber C. Kimball, and others of the Twelve Apostles remained in the temple both day and night, sleeping no more than about four hours a night . . . . As they turned their eyes toward their western migration, they were bolstered in faith and secure in the knowledge that their families were eternally sealed together. Tear-stained faces, ready to move on after burying a child or spouse on America's vast prairie, were resolute largely because of the assurances contained in the ordinances they had received in the temple."[4] Consider the comparison chart on page 14.

God will not be mocked

Too many people attend the temple for the wrong reasons or with the wrong attitude. Some people attend the temple even though they are not worthy because they don't want to disrupt their wedding plans to properly take care of a past indiscretion. Some worry what other people would think if they knew their problem. But the Lord should be considered above family and friends. (And He already knows your problem.) Don't mock Him by entering His house unworthily. President Spencer W. Kimball said, "Remember, God is in his heavens. . . . Those of us who break his commandments will regret and suffer in remorse and pain. God will not be mocked. Man has his free agency, it is sure, but remember, GOD WILL NOT BE MOCKED. (See D&C 63:58.)"[5]

Making temple covenants and then breaking them is serious. Generally speaking, an endowed member of the Church could receive a harsher punishment for certain wrong-doings than an unendowed member would for the same discretion. Once you enter the temple covenants, you are held to a higher standard. After you have received the ordinances of the temple and have covenanted with Heavenly Father, it is too late to go back. Do not enter into the temple covenants lightly.

The Right Attitude to Have When Preparing for the Temple	The Wrong Attitude to Have When Preparing for the Temple
• I want to know how to get back to Heavenly Father.	• I want to see what goes on behind the recommend desk.
• I want to have the opportunity to gain knowledge about where I came from, why I'm here, and where I can go after I die.	• I am only participating in the endowment ceremony because if I don't, they won't let me get married in the temple.
• Even if I don't understand it the first time, I am willing to return to the temple.	• My future husband will tell me what the temple is about, so I don't have to prepare.
• I want to be with my family forever.	• If I attend the temple, maybe it will teach me things that will give me a testimony.
• I want to make covenants with Heavenly Father.	• Even though I'm not worthy, I will go anyway. It will be all right.
• I'm not worried about wearing garments because all my clothing can be worn with them anyway.	• If I think the temple ceremony is weird, I'm not ever going back.
• I will return to the temple as often as I can.	• Wearing temple garments isn't going to allow me to wear the clothing I like, so I'm not going to wear my garments *all* the time.
• I want the temple garment to be a protection to me and a reminder of my temple covenants.	• I don't want to go to the temple, but I will because my family wants me to.

The Holy Spirit of Promise

When we make covenants in the temple (including the marriage covenant), we are entering a two-way promise with the Lord. If we keep the covenants we make there and keep the commandments, the Lord *has* to give us the blessings promised. These blessings can come to us on earth and in heaven, and they can enrich our lives and marriages.

These blessings can only be dispensed if both sides keep their promise. (The Lord will *always* keep His end of the bargain, so it is left up to us if we are to receive blessings.) He said, "I the Lord am bound when ye do what I say, but when ye do not what I say, ye have no promise" (D&C 82:10). Notice that He said when we don't do what we promised Him, He cannot give us the blessings. Not all of the couples who have been sealed in the temple will have an eternal marriage. Merely being sealed in the temple does not guarantee an eternal marriage. The Lord said, "Many are called but few are chosen. And why are they not chosen? Because their hearts are set so much upon the things of this world, and aspire to the honors of men" (D&C 121:34–35). This can happen if either or both of the spouses become unworthy and do not repent. If they do not repent, their marriage will not be sealed upon by the Holy Spirit of Promise (D&C 76:50–54), and they will not be husband and wife in the next life.

Notes
1. Widtsoe, *Discourses*, 416
2. *Our Heritage,* 2.
3. Webb, *Friend*, 26.
4. *Our Heritage,* 60–61.
5. Kimball, *Ensign.*

CHAPTER 3

Secret or *Sacred?*

You've probably heard the saying, "The temple is not *secret*, it's *sacred*." It refers to the assumption (usually made by non–Latter-day Saints) that the reason that only LDS members with a temple recommend can participate in the temple ceremonies is that they're "secret." That belief insinuates that because the temple is not open to everyone, we have something to hide.

Is the temple "exclusive"?

So, why isn't the temple open to everyone? If it were open to everyone, wouldn't that stop people from saying untrue things about the temple? I would say not. For example, consider the large quantity of general information about the Church that *is* available to the public, yet the Church and even its basic doctrines are constantly misrepresented in the media. (How many times have you had to correct someone who believes that you must be a polygamist because you are LDS?) So many misconceptions are circulating that the Church even has a specific spot on its website dedicated to clarifying incorrect statements published about the Church in the media.

The reason the temple is not open to everyone is not that the Church (or better stated, the Lord) wants to exclude people. The Lord wants *everyone* to be able to come to the temple. He invites *anyone* who will do the necessary things (baptism, obedience to the commandments, and so forth) to be worthy to enter His house and receive the blessings there.

Swine and steak

Why can't my non-LDS friend witness my marriage in the temple? She's a good person.

As stated previously, the Lord wants everyone to make themselves worthy to enter the temple. This requires a testimony and obedience to the commandments. The Lord does not keep people from attending the temple—people inadvertently prevent their own admittance. That statement may sound harsh, but let me explain.

Consider a person who (for whatever reason) cannot obtain a temple recommend but wishes to attend the temple with a temple-worthy family member. (This can be someone who isn't a member of the Church, an inactive member, or a member who is not temple worthy.) If he rejects gospel principles, such as the restoration of the gospel, baptism, obedience, tithing, or the Word of Wisdom, he would not be ready to learn the layered meanings of the temple ceremonies. If someone is not willing to make baptismal covenants, how are they expected to make (and keep) the higher covenants made with Heavenly Father during the endowment ceremony?

Someone who rejects the basic principles of the gospel most likely would not have the respect and reverence for the sacredness of the temple that one who believes in the gospel would. (And even if they did, they still need to obey the Lord by being baptized and keeping the commandments.) Have you ever shared a touching, perhaps spiritual, personal experience with someone, only to have him laugh or make light of it because he did not understand what your experience meant to you? How did that make you feel?

The Lord calls this "casting pearls before swine." He taught, "Give not that which is holy unto the dogs, neither cast ye your pearls before swine, lest they trample them under their feet, and turn again and rend you" (Matthew 7:6). He's not calling non–Latter-day Saints or members who are not temple worthy dogs or swine. He is using a metaphor to teach us not to give something precious to someone who wouldn't know what to do with it.

Letting someone who isn't a member of the Church in the temple to witness or participate in a ceremony would be like giving an infant food that is meant for adults. Would you feed a six-month-old baby a steak? Of course not, because the baby's body is not old enough to digest it. The Lord said, "I have fed you with milk, and not with meat: for hitherto ye were not able *to bear it,* neither yet now are ye able" (1 Corinthians 3:2). We must learn about the gospel and the temple "line upon line and precept upon precept" (Isaiah 28:10, 13; see also 2 Nephi 28:30, D&C 98:12, and D&C 128:21).

Use thoughtfulness and sensitivity

There are many reasons certain people can attend the temple and others cannot. Regardless of the circumstances, it is best to carefully explain to anyone who is hurt by not being allowed in the temple the boundaries the Lord has set for temple attendance. It is also a good idea to follow that with an explanation of why a temple marriage is important to *you*. At some temples, workers will sit with anyone who is waiting outside the temple during a wedding and answer questions and may even give them a tour of the grounds.

The gospel principles are beautiful in their simplicity, but if each lesser concept is not accepted, the deeper ones cannot be understood.

CHAPTER 4

Mistaken Ideas People Have

about the Temple

Since the temple ceremonies are not usually discussed, people (both members and non–Latter-day Saints) sometimes develop incorrect ideas about what temple worship is about. Some adopt incorrect terms for temple worship. The following are a few examples to give you an idea.

Misconception #1: The inside of an LDS temple is like the inside of a Catholic cathedral.

I think one of the most common misconceptions people have about our temples is that they are like cathedrals; that is, the inside of the temple is one cavernous, chapel-like room. Most people unfamiliar with the Church or temple worship are surprised to learn that the temple comprises many smaller rooms. If you have the chance, attend a temple open house before you receive your endowment (and bring a non-LDS friend).

Thanks to President Gordon B. Hinckley, temples have been brought to the people. More than fifty temples have been built since President Hinckley became the president of the Church. This increase in temple-building has given not only LDS members access to a temple that they normally wouldn't have, but it has also allowed thousands of non-LDS people the chance to participate in a temple open house and be exposed to the wonderful experience of being inside a temple. When a temple is built, an open house is held for a few weeks before it is dedicated. During an open house, *anyone* can take a guided tour of the temple. (They even let the media and politicians in.) In my opinion, this helps to dispel rumors and generate interest and respect amongst our non-LDS neighbors.

Misconception #2: Once you're in the temple, you can "roam around" the interior. I have taught young women (in more than one ward) who make this assumption. They think that once you receive your temple recommend, you are allowed to wander through the temple to "see what everything looks like." When we go to the temple, we have a specific reason we're there: to participate in one or more ordinances. There isn't a reason to "roam around" the temple. If you participate in all the ordinances, you will have seen most of the interior of the temple.

Misconception #3: "My fiancé is taking me through the temple." It is incorrect to state that your fiancé or husband will be "taking you through the temple." He will be participating in the endowment ceremony, but you will not be sitting with him, and he will not be your temple escort. He will, however, participate in the veil ceremony with you (this is discussed later).

Misconception #4: Obtaining doctrinal knowledge is a man's responsibility. Women are "naturally spiritual" and therefore don't need to study the gospel or prepare for the temple. As I've mentioned before, some young women are under the impression that if they have a question about the temple, they'll just ask their future husband about it. Little do they know, even though their future husband has most likely been on a mission, he probably is as clueless about the temple ceremony as they are. I believe that even some members of the Church have the entire endowment ceremony memorized but don't know what it means or how to apply it to their lives.

Misconception #5: If you are a woman, you have to be either preparing for a mission or engaged or married to receive the ordinances of the temple. A single woman can receive the temple ordinances, but this path is not for everyone. Generally speaking, a girl right out of high school or even in her early twenties is not emotionally mature or spiritually ready to immediately take on the responsibility of being endowed. (Of course there are exceptions. Please don't write me a letter explaining how you, or someone you know, are the exception.) Carefully consult the Lord through prayer, and work closely with your bishop before making a decision like this one. If your bishop tells you he feels it is not right for you, heed his counsel.

Misconception #6: The endowment ceremony consists of an instructor giving lectures about the mysteries of life after death. I know the temple is sometimes referred to as "the Lord's university," but it is important to understand that the temple ceremonies are not a series of classes. As you'll discover, the endowment ceremony is the same ceremony every time you go to the temple. In the temple, you learn by careful study and prayer, the Holy Ghost, and through the gospel language of symbols; it is not by listening to various lectures.

Misconception #7: "I'm taking out my endowments." In the LDS culture, many people use this phrase to describe the first time they attend the temple. It is correct to say, "I will *receive* my own endowment" or "I will *receive* my endowment" (also notice that the word "endowment" is not plural). The phrase "taking out my endowments" implies two things: (1) you are somehow collecting object(s) at the temple that you will take home and (2) there is more than one endowment. Both are misconceptions.

There are many more misconceptions people have about temple worship. If you have any questions, direct them to your bishop, branch president, or stake president. He will be happy to discuss them with you.

CHAPTER 5

Temple

Etiquette

I believe that while on the temple grounds and inside the temple, you can show respect for yourself, others around you, and, most important, the Lord, by keeping the following tips in mind.

Turn off your cell phone. You may bring your pager or cell phone into the temple, but you need to turn it off and leave it in your locker while you're participating in the ceremonies.

When you're participating in an ordinance, any vocalization besides an occasional whisper is inappropriate. You'd be surprised how many people can be distracted when one person constantly whispers to another. It can take away from the spirit. A young woman, distraught over the sudden death of her spouse, may have come to the temple for peace and guidance from the Lord. Instead, she hears all about how your sister-in-law got a speeding ticket and how fun your recent vacation to Mexico was.

Leave all worldly cares outside the temple. As noted above, talking about mundane things inside the temple is not a good idea. Hopefully you're at the temple because you want to feel the spirit, seek special guidance from the Lord, learn something about the gospel, or do work for the dead. That can hardly be accomplished when you've got your mind on where you have to be at four o'clock later that day.

Wear appropriate clothing to the temple. You're going to worship in the Lord's house, not hang out at your friend Michelle's house. Wear Sunday-appropriate clothing that is modest, clean, and ironed. Do not wear footwear that resembles a flip-flop.

Leave your treats and snacks at home. Or at least leave them in the car. I have a friend who swears she once saw a man eating fried chicken during an endowment session. I know someone else who said when he volunteered to clean the temple, he vacuumed popcorn off the floor of the endowment room. I guess if you have a medical condition (like diabetes), having a candy or two on hand isn't a bad idea. But leave the popcorn and the Colonel at home.

Respect the temple grounds. This can be accomplished by refraining from (amongst other things) playing tag, shouting, littering, sleeping, making out, swimming in any bodies of water, or picking the flowers on the grounds. (Anyone who thinks this paragraph was a waste of space hasn't been to Temple Square.)

Keep in mind, these are only a few examples. Use common sense regarding your conduct while you are at the temple; it will make your temple experience (and the experience of those people around you) more meaningful.

CHAPTER 6

Temple
Garments

Armor of God

The temple garment serves three purposes: "It is a reminder of the sacred covenants made with the Lord in His holy house, a protective covering for the body, and a symbol of the modest of dress and living that should characterize the lives of all the humbles followers of Christ. It is written that 'the white garment symbolizes purity and helps assure modesty, respect for the attributes of God, and . . . [is] a token of what Paul regarded as taking upon one the whole armor of God (Ephesians 6:13) . . . Garments bear several simple marks of orientation toward the gospel principles of obedience, truth, life, and discipleship in Christ.' "[1]

What should (or shouldn't) I do with my temple garments?

The first time you attend the temple, you will need to bring an unopened package of garments. Buy them when you purchase your temple ceremony clothing, and keep them in your temple bag. Temple garments and temple clothing can be purchased from a church distribution center. Victor L. Brown stated: *"It is not appropriate to wear or try on marked garments before being endowed.* However, Beehive Clothing distribution centers have unmarked garments that may be tried on for sizing purposes. Those coming to the temple to be endowed are not to wear their garments to the temple, but should carry them in a package."[2]

I have been taught by seminary teachers, my parents, a former bishop, and temple workers that garments are to be treated with respect and are never to be altered in any way. In my opinion this includes, but is not limited to, pinning, rolling back, purposely shrinking in the laundry, or leaving them on the floor. Do not take off your garment top so you can wear a shirt or dress that is not modest, and do not purposely buy smaller sizes. Only wearing your garment bottoms does not count as "properly" wearing garments. Making a permanent commitment now to wear modest clothing can eliminate any temptation to alter the garment.

Elder Boyd K. Packer stated in his classic book *The Holy Temple*, "The garment represents sacred covenants. It fosters modesty and becomes a shield and a protection to the wearer. . . . Only clothing that is immodest or extreme in style would be incompatible with wearing the garment."[3]

Some activities require the removal of garments. They are lovingly referred to as "the S's" (showering, swimming, some sports, and sexual activity). Your bishop or your parents can go over those with you in greater depth.

This information is just the basics about garments. If you are interested in learning more, please refer to the back of this book (in a chapter titled "Further Light and Knowledge") for some excellent books and articles.

Notes

1. Marshall, *Encyclopedia of Mormonism,* 2:534.
2. Brown, *New Era*, 30; emphasis added.
3. Packer, *The Holy Temple*, 75.

CHAPTER 7

Why Symbolism?

A foreign language?

Elder John A. Widtsoe said: "We live in a world of symbols. No man or woman can come out of the temple endowed as he should be, unless he has seen, beyond the symbol, the mighty realities for which the symbols stand."[1]

Did you know that the temple ceremonies are conducted in a language you are probably not familiar with? Symbolism is a foreign language to many members of the Church. Fortunately there are many helpful resources for those members who are not familiar with it.

Other religions use symbolism heavily as part of their worship rituals (have you ever been to a Catholic Mass?). However, Sunday worship for LDS members does not involve a lot of visible gospel symbolism, with one exception: the sacrament. Some members of the Church take the sacrament without really understanding the symbols it represents.

In remembrance of Him

Bread and Water

The Savior instituted the sacrament in conjunction with the last hours of his mortal ministry. "And as they were eating, Jesus took bread, and blessed it, and brake it, and gave it to the disciples, and said, Take, eat; this is my body. And he took the cup, and gave thanks, and gave it to them, saying, Drink ye all of it; For this is my blood of the new testament, which is shed for many for the remission of sins" (Matthew 26:26–28).

We consume the bread and water both to renew our covenants we have already made with the Lord and to convey the idea that we are "taking upon the name of Christ" (Mosiah 5:8; Alma 34:38; Moroni 4:3). We do this by literally making the symbols of the bread and water part of our bodies and lives. The words of the sacrament prayer are specific about what we need to do when we partake of it. We are commanded to do three things:

- Eat the bread and drink the water in remembrance of the body and blood of the Savior.
- Witness to God that we are "willing to take upon them the name of [His] Son and always remember him."
- Keep His commandments.

Our reward is to "always have his spirit" to be with us (Moroni 4:3).

Note: The Savior is also referred to in many instances throughout the scriptures as both "living bread" or "bread of life" and also "living water" (John 4:14; 6:32, 51). Bread and water can sustain our physical life, but the Savior (as "*living* bread and water") can bring eternal life.

Since most members of the Church (and ironically those who have been brought up in the Church) are accustomed to the sacrament service being the only symbolic rite they participate in, the symbolic rites of the temple can be confusing to them. Some people have told me that during their first temple experience, they wondered if the temple ceremony was even related to the same religion as the one they attend on Sunday. If they had understood prior to attending the temple that the Lord teaches His most profound truths by way of symbolism, they would have welcomed the way in which the ceremonies are presented.

Why symbols?

Why doesn't Heavenly Father just come right out and tell us what he wants us to know? I imagine that would stretch the endowment ceremony from roughly ninety minutes to hours and maybe even days.

The use of symbols can be related to how and why the Savior used parables. Those who have the spiritual "ears to hear and eyes to see" will understand the message (Matthew 13:10–15). Symbolic messages can also have different layers of meaning.

I had a seminary teacher who explained that learning about the gospel can be compared to recreating on a lake or in the ocean. One person can water ski along the surface of the water, a second person can snorkel just below the surface, and a third person can dive to the deepest depths. The temple ceremonies can also be understood on different levels, depending on the symbols used and the understanding the participant has.

Symbols in and on the temple

Obviously I'm not going to go into *too* much detail here, but I do want to give you some basic examples. For example, did you know that body parts, clothing, colors, and even the rooms themselves are symbolic in temple worship?

Think about when a person offers a prayer. In Alonzo Gaskill's book *The Lost Language of Symbolism*, Brother Gaskill mentions that folding one's arms and bowing one's head is a symbolic act of submission, humility, and reverence.[2] He also mentions articles of clothing such as shoes or slippers. He said, "Shoes have . . . symbolic connotations in scripture and temple worship [and can symbolize] . . . entrance into a hallowed place, and covenant making." He then mentions that in Bible times, "To be barefoot and then receive shoes again served as a symbol of . . . regaining of one's social standing."[3]

It is common knowledge that colors can represent different moods or ideas. Reds can invoke feelings of anger, warmth, or even hunger. Red can also be a symbol of blood and of the Atonement. As a symbol of the blood He shed for us, Jesus Christ will wear a red robe when He comes again (Isaiah 63:2; D&C 133:48).

Blues can suggest cleanliness and promote restfulness, but the color blue is even associated with feelings of depression ("the blues"). It can also be a symbol of divinity since the sky is blue. The color representing the Young Women value Divine Nature is blue (2 Peter 1:4–7). I have noticed that often in Renaissance- and Medieval-era paintings, Mary, the mother of Jesus, is clothed in blue robes. This is a symbol of her divinity.

In the temple, patrons wear white because it is a symbol of purity and worthiness. The use of white as a symbol of purity and worthiness is an image repeated often in the scriptures (Isaiah 1:18; 2 Nephi 5:21). Heavenly beings, including Heavenly Father and Jesus Christ, are often described as wearing white clothing (Mark 9:3; 3 Nephi 11:8; JS–H 1:31).

Even rooms inside the temple are symbolic. For example, in the Salt Lake Temple, several rooms are used to convey the idea of progression back to the presence of God. Each room represents a different world or kingdom (telestial, terrestrial, and celestial). Each room is placed higher than the previous one. The temple patron must physically climb higher and higher until he or she reaches the celestial room, which represents the celestial kingdom and the presence of Heavenly Father (see D&C 76).

The room in the temple that holds the baptismal font is symbolic. Whenever possible, the baptismal font is located below ground-level, in the basement of the temple. The font itself and its location symbolize the grave and death. The water in the font is a symbol of Christ (Jeremiah 2:13, 17:13) being buried or immersed in the water and then being brought out of it is a symbol of being resurrected by the power of the Atonement (D&C 128:12–13). Being immersed in water is also an obvious symbol of becoming free from the stains of sin.

Now let's talk about the exterior of the temple. The Nauvoo and Salt Lake temples have exterior symbolism that is recognizable to members and non–Latter-day Saints alike. If you've ever visited Temple Square in Salt Lake City, you've probably noticed the various symbols that the pioneers carved into the granite exterior of the temple. You have probably been told what the star, moon, and sun stones represent (D&C 76). Did you know there are stars in the configuration of the Big Dipper located on the Salt Lake Temple (situated on the central, upper west tower)? What about the "All-Seeing Eye"? Matthew B. Brown and Paul Thomas Smith, in their book *Symbols in Stone,* discuss how the All-Seeing Eye "represents God's ability to see all things (see D&C 88:41; 130:7) . . . [and] heavenly eyes are said to represent one who is filled with 'light and knowledge' (D&C 77:4)."[4] (The All-Seeing Eye is also depicted in other church buildings such as the St. George Tabernacle in St. George, Utah.) The Big

Dipper has been used for centuries by ancient and modern navigators to locate the North Star and to consequently find their way home. It is appropriate that a symbol of how to find your way home is located on the temple, a structure where we learn how to find our way back to our heavenly home. It is a symbol of where to find answers for those who are spiritually lost.[5]

Looking beyond the mark (Jacob 4:14)

During the time of Christ, the local Jewish leaders frequently worshipped in the temple. They participated in rituals (sacrificing of animals) that typified the sacrifice Jesus Christ would make. They celebrated the Passover (Exodus 12). Jehovah (it is important to remember that it was Jehovah) instituted the Passover to teach the Hebrews about the atonement. Jehovah commanded the Hebrews to kill a young, male lamb "without blemish" and then paint the blood on the outside of their doorway (Exodus 12:5, 7). Any home that bore the mark of the blood on the doorway was "passed over" by the plague of death that the Lord Jehovah sent to Egypt. "For I will pass through the land . . . and will smite all the firstborn . . . And the blood shall be to you a token upon the houses . . . and when I see the blood, I will pass over you, and the plague shall not be upon you to destroy you" (Exodus 12:12–13). The point: the Atonement and subsequently Jesus Christ (which both the lamb and the blood of the lamb signify) "saves us from both physical and spiritual death."[6]

The Pharisees and Sadducees were precise in their worship rituals, but the actual message that the symbolic rites were trying to convey (the Atonement) was lost on most of them. It is deeply ironic that the Savior of the World completed the sacred act of the Atonement on the cross (in part because the Jewish leaders themselves called for his death and pleaded to the Romans to carry it out) during the *very* time they, the Pharisees and Sadducees, were celebrating the Passover (Matthew 26–27).

Likewise, we must be careful not to "look beyond the mark" (Jacob 4:14) in both our membership in the Church and in our own symbolic temple worship. The ancient Jews attended the temple and studied the words of the prophets, yet they still were not prepared for the Savior's coming because they did not have "ears to hear" (Matthew 11:15).

Jesus called the local Jewish leaders hypocrites because they obeyed the rites and rituals to the letter of the law, but inwardly they were wicked and did not believe. He said they were "like unto whited sepulchres, which indeed appear beautiful outward, but are within full of dead *men's* bones, and of all uncleanness" (Matthew 23:27).

We need to ensure we are not hypocrites in our modern-day temple worship so that we can embody the teachings of the gospel and be prepared for the Savior's Second Coming.

Notes

1. Widtsoe, *Utah Genealogical and Historical Magazine,* 62.
2. Gaskill, 2.
3. Ibid, 3.
4. Brown and Smith, 140.
5. Ibid, 156.
6. *Old Testament: Gospel Doctrine Teacher's Manual,* 14.

CHAPTER 8

Our First *Parents*

The first temple

A temple can be defined as an intersection between heaven and earth. It is the only place where man can dwell with God and where God can teach man eternal truths. Many prophets, such as Moses, have used mountain tops as temples because mountain tops are, literally and symbolically, where heaven and earth touch (Exodus 3–4, Moses). The phrase "Mountain of the Lord" refers to a temple for that reason (Isaiah 2:2–3). Temples have taken many forms through the ages, but it is important to understand (in reference to the endowment ceremony) that the first temple was not the portable tabernacle the Israelites toted through the wilderness, or even Mount Sinai. The first temple was the Garden of Eden itself.[1]

The events surrounding Adam and Eve are crucial to both our salvation and our exaltation, so naturally it is a crucial part of the endowment ceremony. The story of Adam and Eve must be understood on different levels. As with many scriptural accounts, this can be seen as both a historical record and as a metaphor. In the temple, we can learn of our own existence and exaltation vicariously through Adam and Eve's journey.

"Return to His presence"

"When our Heavenly Father placed Adam and Eve on this earth, He did so with the purpose in mind of teaching them how to return to His presence. Our Father promised a Savior to redeem them from their fallen condition. He gave to them the plan of salvation and told them to teach their children faith in Jesus Christ and repentance. Further, Adam and his posterity were commanded by God to be baptized, to receive the Holy Ghost, and to enter into the order of the Son of God."[2]

"Three pillars of eternity"

"Before we can comprehend the Atonement of Christ . . . we must first understand the Fall of Adam. And before we can understand the Fall of Adam, we must first understand the Creation. These three crucial components of the plan of salvation relate to each other."[3]

According to Bruce R. McConkie, the "three pillars of eternity" are the Creation, the Fall, and the Atonement.[4] These three events give each of us salvation. In Heavenly Father's infinite wisdom, He created the plan of exaltation. He told Moses, "For behold—this is my work and my glory to bring to pass the immortality and eternal life of man" (Moses 1:39). The fall of Adam and Eve made it possible for mankind to feel pain, have joy, and experience free agency, but it also made it possible for men to die both physically and spiritually. After the Fall occurred, mankind was an enemy to God. In Mosiah 3:19 we read, "For the natural man is an enemy to God, and has been from the fall of Adam, and will be, forever and ever, unless he yields to the enticings of the Holy Spirit, and putteth off the natural man and becometh a saint through the atonement of Christ the Lord." That is why the atonement of Jesus Christ is necessary. "For as in Adam all die, even so in Christ shall all be made alive" (1 Corinthians 15:22).

A vicarious work

When we return to the temple to do work for the dead, we act as proxy for them. That is, we participate in the temple ordinance with that person's name, and, consequently, the ordinance is done as though that person had received it herself. The Atonement was performed by Jesus Christ as a proxy for all of mankind. The same can be said about the Fall. Adam and Eve acted as a proxy for all mankind when they fell from God's presence. The Fall was a necessary act in order to bring mankind eternal glory. "Adam fell that men might be, and men are that they have joy" (2 Nephi 2:25).

In the Salt Lake Temple, a temple patron must pass through different rooms representing various worlds and kingdoms. For instance, a person must pass from one room representing the Garden of Eden (God's presence) into the next room representing the lone and dreary world (the condition of the world after the Fall). It is noteworthy to add that the temple patron must walk upward on a ramp or stairs from the garden room to the world room. I believe this suggests to the mind that even something referred to as "the Fall" was actually a necessary step toward eternal glory and Heavenly Father's presence (which ends in the celestial room).

"Opposition in all things"

The Fall of Adam made it possible for mankind to experience good by overcoming evil. Lehi told his son Jacob, "For it must needs be, that there is an opposition in all things. If not so, my first-born in the wilderness, righteousness could not be brought to pass, neither wickedness, neither holiness nor misery, neither good nor bad. Wherefore, all things must needs be a compound in one; wherefore, if it should be one body it must needs remain as dead, having no life neither death, nor corruption nor incorruption, happiness nor misery, neither sense nor insensibility" (2 Nephi 2:11).

There are several instances of opposition in the scriptural account of the Creation and the Fall. One notable instance is the two trees mentioned in the Garden of Eden. One was the tree of knowledge of good and evil (Genesis 2:9, Moses 3:17), and its opposite was the tree of life (Moses 4:28). (Also compare this tree of life and its fruit with the tree of life and its fruit mentioned in Lehi's Dream [1 Nephi 8:10–12].) According to Brother Gaskill, "The two trees represent our two choices: obedience to God or obedience to our own will. Partaking of each tree has its own consequence."[5] Brother Gaskill also refers to the following observations that I have organized into the following comparison chart:

Tree of Knowledge of Good and Evil	Tree of Life
• Fruit tasted bitter	• Fruit tasted sweet
• Fruit brings death	• Fruit brings eternal life
• Our own agency/natural man	• Obedience to God
• Bitter experiences	• Sweet forgiveness from God
• Can represent Satan	• Represents Jesus Christ

Even though the tree of knowledge of Good and evil is associated with death, bitterness, and even Satan, partaking of its fruit was not necessarily a bad thing. Partaking of the fruit brought mankind agency and the chance to become like Heavenly Father.

The Fall and the Atonement are opposites in the sense that one caused us to fall from God's presence, and one gives us the chance to return to it. However, both are required for us to progress, and they both ultimately have the same purpose. "And the Messiah cometh in the fulness of time, that he may redeem the children of men from the fall. And because that they are redeemed from the fall they have become free forever, knowing good from evil; to act for themselves and not to be acted upon, save it be by the punishment of the law at the great and last day, according to the commandments which God hath given" (2 Nephi 2:26).

Notes

1. Brown, *Symbolism on the Early Temples of the Restoration*, 14.
2. Benson, *Tambuli*, 2.
3. Nelson, *Ensign*, 33.
4. McConkie, *A New Witness for the Articles of Faith*, 81.

CHAPTER 9

What to Expect Your First Time
at the Temple

Finally

Let's learn a little about the temple ceremonies. Don't be afraid to participate in the temple ceremonies. Nervousness accompanies any first-time experience, but you're going to the house of the Lord. *There is nothing in His house that you need to worry about.* The Lord said, "Look unto me in every thought; doubt not, fear not" (D&C 6:36).

You are not going to fully understand the ceremonies the first time through, so don't worry. To understand it, you will need to go back. You can gain a little more understanding from the temple ceremonies each time you participate in it. Going to the temple is like watching a favorite movie over and over. The more you see the same movie, the more you understand the plot. Before long, you will be saying, "I never noticed that before; that's neat."

Be spiritually minded

Elder Russell M. Nelson said, "The temple endowment was given by revelation. Thus it is best understood by revelation."[1] Careful prayer and meditation can open doors to personal understanding that studying books can-not. Joseph Smith said the endowment was "of things spiritual, and to be received only by the spiritual mind-ed."[2] Following that example is crucial to receiving per-sonal revelation both in and out of the temple.

Temple rookies

Don't worry about somehow "getting lost" in the temple. You're not going to end up in a broom closet or anything like that. Not only do the temple workers pin a card to your clothing that indicates you're a rookie, they let you bring someone with you to escort you through the process.

The person you choose to be your escort needs to be a female family member or friend who is endowed and holds a current temple recommend. She (along with the temple workers themselves) will help you during your first experience at the temple. If you do not have an escort in mind, the temple will provide one for you. (As noted in chapter 4, if you have a fiancé or husband, he will not be your escort but will be present during the ceremony.)

The ceremonies

The first time you attend the temple, you will partici-pate in both the washing and anointing, or initiatory or-dinance, and the endowment ceremony. In the initiatory, you will receive and learn about the symbolism of temple garments, along with many blessings. Listen carefully to the beautiful promises Heavenly Father has offered to you if you remain worthy. At a certain point, you will be given your new name (Revelation 2:17), which is (among other things) a symbol of the covenants you are about to make with Heavenly Father. (Remember how Jacob was renamed Israel after he made covenants with the Lord?

See Genesis 32:28.) Then you will be brought into the ordinance room to begin the endowment.

Since this is your first experience in the temple, it is customary for the temple workers to seat you and your female escort on the front row so you can easily see the presentation of the endowment. As part of the symbolism of this portion of the ceremony, women are seated on one side of the room and men on the other. It is only in the celestial room, which represents the celestial kingdom, that men and women can mingle with each other.

The endowment ceremony itself consists of two different elements: the presentation of the drama and the covenant-making process. Your escort will help you participate in the ceremony. At the end of the endowment, you will be required to go through the veil of the temple, which leads into the celestial room. If you attend the temple for the first time while engaged or married, your fiancé or husband will participate in the veil ceremony with you. He will only participate in this portion of the ceremony the first time you attend the temple.

Once you've completed the veil ceremony, you will be inside the celestial room. In this room, it is appropriate to sit and ponder, pray, feel the spirit, or speak of things you normally wouldn't outside the temple. This is a good opportunity to quietly talk about things you learned while participating in the ceremony. You can also ask temple workers any questions you may have.

Remember, the first time you go, you don't need to understand everything you're participating in. You will have temple workers and your escort to help you. I believe that the reason we don't grasp and remember everything the first time we attend the temple is part of the reason we have the opportunity to return to the temple. We can gain a greater insight into the meaning of the ceremony while giving someone on the other side of the veil the opportunity to receive the temple ordinances.

Going back for more

The next time you return to the temple, you will be acting as proxy from someone who has died. You can do any one of the ordinances or choose to do several. Generally speaking, most people choose to participate in the endowment ceremony. Many couples opt to participate in sealing sessions at the temple as part of an occasional date night with their spouse. If you're going with a female friend, try doing initiatories or even baptisms for the dead.

Facts about the endowment

Even though the endowment ceremony is the same ceremony every time you go and is the same in every temple, it may be presented differently in various temples.

For example, the Salt Lake and Manti, Utah, temples present the endowment ceremony live, meaning with live actors instead of a video presentation. In these two temples, you would "progress," meaning you would change rooms during the ceremony (creation room, garden room, world room/telestial room, terrestrial room, celestial room). In other temples, such as the Jordan River Temple, you would remain in one ordinance room the entire presentation of the endowment. In yet other temples, such as the Idaho Falls Temple and the newly rebuilt Nauvoo Temple, you "progress" through different rooms, but the endowment is given via a video presentation. (A fun thing to do, if it is possible, is to travel with your husband or friends to as many temples as you can to experience the different ways the endowment is presented.)

The point is, it doesn't matter how the endowment is presented, because the message is the same. In fact, the manner in which the endowment ceremony is presented has been modified several times since Joseph Smith revealed it in 1844. The most recent changes were instituted in 1990, and a change to the initiatory was instituted in early 2005. According to John D. Charles, in his informative book *Endowed from on High*, the endowment ceremony first presented by Joseph Smith lasted more than *five hours*, whereas our modern ceremony lasts an average of ninety minutes. Why was it changed? The cultural needs and understandings of the Saints have changed since the 1840s, and under the direction of living prophets, the way the endowment ceremony was presented has changed with them. The way the endowment is presented now may change again in the future, if the current prophet deems it necessary.[3]

Notes
1. Nelson, *Ensign*, 1.
2. *Teachings of the Prophet Joseph Smith*, 237.
3. Charles, 31–32.

Conclusion

I hope this book has been encouraging and informative without being overwhelming. Remember, like Adam, we *can* accomplish the things the Lord wants us to do (in this case, attending the temple) without the knowledge of *why* we're doing it—just based on the fact that God asks us to. But this book is designed to show you how to begin to learn more about the temple and, consequently, how to apply it to your life.

I hope you will be able to share your experience of learning about the temple with a parent or close friend. Learning about the temple is not merely for those who are preparing for it. It is an ongoing process and is equally beneficial to those who have already received the ordinances. I challenge you to read this book (and any other references) again, *after* you have attended the temple. More and more concepts will make sense to you, and your eyes will be opened. As with every gospel principle, after you study, you can pray to Heavenly Father for a confirmation through the Holy Ghost that it's a true principle (James 1:5). The Lord said, "Ask and it shall be given you; Seek and ye shall find; Knock and it shall be opened unto you" (Matthew 7:7).

I hope you will read the next section, "Further Light and Knowledge," and find joy in learning about the house of the Lord.

APPENDIX 1

Further Light
and

Seek ye out of the best books words of wisdom; seek learning, even by study and also by faith.

—D&C 88:118

This section is not meant to overwhelm you. You do not *have* to read all of these books or magazines or watch any of the DVDs listed in order to attend the temple. This section is merely a list of suggestions if you wish to know more.

Of course there are more references available than are listed. These are just a few to help you begin. While all of these references are great to read, I would like to highlight a few of them and help you choose which books to start with.

I would recommend starting with the scriptural references listed in this section. If you read nothing else, read the scriptural references.

I *highly* recommend purchasing the magazine *Temples of The Church of Jesus Christ of Latter-day Saints*, because besides having wonderful interior photographs of various temples, it has entire articles dedicated to garments, salvation of the dead, and commonly asked questions. This magazine is modestly priced and can be purchased through the Church Distribution Center. The same could be said of the booklet adapted from Boyd K. Packer's book *The Holy Temple*. It was revised in 2002 and now has interior photographs of some of the newer temples, such as the Vernal Utah Temple, the Columbia River Falls Temple, and the San Diego Temple. It is now called "Preparing to Enter the Holy Temple" and is available at LDS bookstores and through the Church Distribution Center. The above mentioned references are wonderful sources of information for a beginner.

Then I recommend reading the books *Youth and the Temple* by temple artist Chad S. Hawkins (a quick 134 pages; read this book even if you aren't a "youth"), *The Holy Temple* by Boyd K. Packer, and *Endowed from on High* by John D. Charles (an even quicker 112 pages). These are great books to begin your study with. Later you might want to try *The Gate of Heaven* by Matthew B. Brown and listen to audio talks or books like *Making Sense of Gospel Symbols* by Alonzo Gaskill or *The Temple and the Atonement* by Truman Madsen. Talks and books on CD are wonderful because you can listen to them in your car while you drive back and forth to work or school.

Since the fall of Adam and Eve is such an important feature of the endowment ceremony, I have included books like *The Plan of Salvation* by Matthew B. Brown, *Eve and the Choice Made in Eden* by Beverly Campbell, *The Savior and the Serpent* by Alonzo Gaskill, and *Doctrinal Details of the Plan of Salvation* by David Ridges. There is a wonderful section on the Fall in *Celestial Symbols* by Allen H. Barber.

Are you confused about gospel symbolism? Besides *Celestial Symbols*, try *The Lost Language of Symbolism* by

Alonzo Gaskill and *Gospel Symbolism* by Joseph Fielding McConkie. They are all great reference books. *Symbols in Stone* by Matthew B. Brown and Paul Thomas Smith is a great book to begin your understanding of symbols because it focuses on the symbols carved into the exterior and used in the interior architecture of the temples in Kirtland, Nauvoo, and Salt Lake City.

Another great way to begin is to watch the DVDs and videos listed at the end of this section. *Between Heaven and Earth* explains the origins and purposes of temples. It features interviews of "temple experts" within the LDS Church, as well as prominent members of other faiths and staff members of prestigious universities, many of which (at the time this video was made) had recently attended the open house for the Boston Temple. *The Mountain of the Lord* is a dramatized version of the events surrounding the building of the Salt Lake Temple. It features the sacrifice the early Saints had to endure to build the temple, and it features beautiful interior shots of the Salt Lake Temple. *Nauvoo: A Temple Reborn* is the actual video presentation that was shown to everyone who toured the rebuilt Nauvoo Temple during its open house in 2002. It also features a segment on why we have temples and shows pictures of the interior of the Nauvoo Temple and clips of members of the Church expressing their thoughts on the temple. All three are available through the Church Distribution Center.

Scriptures to Get You Started

Baptism
1 Corinthians 15:29
Colossians 2:12
Acts 2:38
Romans 6:4
D&C 18:22, 41; 20:37, 73
D&C 124: 28–33, 36
D&C 128:12–13, 17–18
Moses 8:34

Washings and Anointings (Initiatory)
Exodus 29:4; 30:17–21, 29, 31
Leviticus 8:10–12; 14:7–8
Isaiah 1:16
Psalm 73:13
Hebrews 9:10
1 John 2:27
D&C 88:74–75, 85
D&C 124:37–39

The Endowment
Genesis 1–3
Genesis 32:28
Luke 24:49
Revelation 2:17
Mormon 9:12
D&C 20:17-20
D&C 43:16
D&C 84:20–21; 105:11–12
D&C 124:39
Moses 1–3
Abraham 3–5

Sealings
Matthew 16:19
2 Corinth 6:14
D&C 128:14–15
D&C 131:1–8

Suggested Books

Barber, Allen H. *Celestial Symbols: Symbolism in Doctrine, Religious Traditions and Temple Architecture.* Springville, Utah: Horizon Publishers, 2003.

Brown, Matthew B. *The Gate of Heaven: Insights on the Doctrines and Symbols of the Temple.* American Fork, Utah: Covenant Communications, 1999.

Brown, Matthew B. *The Plan of Salvation: Doctrinal Notes and Commentary.* American Fork, Utah: Covenant Communications, 2002.

Brown, Matthew B. and Paul Thomas Smith. *Symbols in Stone: Symbolism on the Early Temples of the Restoration.* American Fork, Utah: Covenant Communications, 1997.

Campbell, Beverly. *Eve and the Choice Made in Eden.* Salt Lake City: Bookcraft, 2003.

Charles, John D. *Endowed from on High: Understanding the Symbols of the Endowment.* Springville, Utah: Horizon Publishers, 1999.

Edmunds, John K. *Through Temple Doors.* Salt Lake City: Bookcraft, 1978 (out of print).

Gaskill, Alonzo. *The Lost Language of Symbolism: An Essential Guide for Recognizing and Interpreting Symbols of the Gospel.* Salt Lake City: Deseret Book, 2003.

Gaskill, Alonzo. *The Savior and the Serpent: Unlocking the Doctrine of the Fall.* Salt Lake City: Deseret Book, 2005.

Hawkins, Chad S. *Youth and the Temple: What You Want to Know and How You Can Prepare.* Salt Lake City: Bookcraft, 2002.

Kimball, Spencer W. *The Miracle of Forgiveness.* Salt Lake City: Bookcraft, 1969.

McConkie, Joseph Fielding. *Gospel Symbolism.* Salt Lake City: Deseret Book, 1985.

Nibley, Hugh. *The Meaning of the Temple.* Provo: FARMS (Foundation for Ancient Research and Mormon Studies), 1984.

Packer, Boyd K. *The Holy Temple.* Salt Lake City: Bookcraft, Inc., 1980.

Ridges, David J. *Doctrinal Details of the Plan of Salvation: From Pre-mortality to Exaltation.* Springville, Utah: CFI, 2005.

Wilcox, S. Michael. *House of Glory: Finding Personal Meaning in the Temple.* Salt Lake City: Deseret Book, 1995.

Magazines and Booklets

Packer, Boyd K. *Preparing to Enter the Holy Temple* (adapted from *The Holy Temple*). Salt Lake City: Intellectual Reserve, Inc. Revised 2002.

Temples of the Church of Jesus Christ of Latter-day Saints. Salt Lake City: *Ensign* of The Church of Jesus Christ of Latter-day Saints, Intellectual Reserve, Inc. 1999.

Talks & Books on CD

Making Sense of Gospel Symbols. By Alonzo Gaskill. Covenant Communications Inc. 2001.

The Temple and the Atonement. By Truman Madsen, Donald W. Parry, M. Catherine Thomas. Provo: Covenant/ FARMS, 1994.

DVDs

Between Heaven and Earth. Intellectual Reserve, Inc., 2002.

The Mountain of the Lord. Intellectual Reserve, Inc., 1993, 2005.

Nauvoo: A Temple Reborn. Intellectual Reserve, Inc., 2002.

APPENDIX 2

Bonus: Temple Wedding *Tips*

Since most girls who read this book will soon prepare for a wedding, let's talk about the wedding day itself. Here are some pitfalls to avoid (and some helpful hints) when planning your temple wedding:

1. Remember to bring your "live ordinance" temple recommend(s) to the temple. Also have your marriage license and temple clothing ready to go. (Sometimes the county will send your license to the temple for you, so you will need to verify how it will get to the temple.) Have everything packed ahead of time in your temple bag so you don't have to worry about where anything is on your wedding day. You will need to bring two endowed brethren over the age of eighteen to act as witnesses to the ceremony (or the temple can provide them). You and your fiancé may have one escort each to assist you in the temple. You may choose an endowed friend or relative of the same gender to act as your escort.

2. Don't buy a wedding dress that is any color other than white. You need to have a white dress for the ceremony. Please avoid off-white, ivory, or cream-colored dresses and dresses with colored ribbons or colored embroidery. Sure, it is "in" to be different, but remember, you're getting married in the temple, which commands the observance of the symbols of purity. After all, wedding dresses are traditionally white to symbolize the purity (virginity) of the bride. Ivory and other colored wedding dresses were similarly created for different reasons (it is appropriate for a pregnant bride to wear ivory to her non-temple wedding ceremony).

You're worthy to enter the temple. That alone makes you different from the world. Wear an all-white wedding dress that is symbolic of your worthiness to be in the house of the Lord. Also keep in mind that embellishments need to be kept to a minimum. Any sheer fabric must be lined, and make sure the train can be bustled. If you *do* decide to buy an ivory-colored wedding dress, don't expect to wear it during your sealing. The temple workers will not allow it, and you would be required to wear your (appropriately all-white) temple dress instead. That outcome could be very embarrassing and upsetting to a bride on her wedding day.

3. Buy a wedding dress that can be comfortably worn over temple garments. Don't alter your sacred temple garments; alter the wedding dress. I would think this would be obvious and wouldn't have to be said, but I have heard of too many instances to leave it out. As has been explained before, never pin back your garments (or opt to not wear the garment top or shrink it in the wash) so that immodest wedding dresses (or any other clothing) can be worn. There are plenty of beautiful, stylish wedding dresses LDS brides can purchase that are "temple ready." (I believe that even bridesmaid dresses for a temple wedding should adhere to the temple garment standards.) To get started, try searching online. There are many choices for LDS brides today. Another option is to alter an immodest wedding dress by adding more fabric to fit the temple standards (example: adding sleeves to a dress that is otherwise modest). If an immodest wedding dress (meaning a dress without sleeves or that has a low back or neckline) is brought to the temple, the temple workers will not allow it to be worn to the ceremony. Short-sleeved dresses are acceptable, but during the ceremony you will be required to wear under your dress a special jacket that extends to your wrists. Also (many brides don't realize this), because a temple wedding is a temple ceremony, you will be wearing your ceremonial temple clothing. Your ceremonial clothing will be worn on top of your wedding dress. (You're essentially substituting your wedding dress for your white temple dress during the ceremony.)

4. Don't plan on a wedding-day hairstyle that requires the veil, flowers, or a tiara to be woven into your hair. You will not be wearing your wedding veil during the sealing ceremony, and it must be able to be removed. Flowers, glitter, tiaras, and other adornments must not be worn during the sealing ceremony. (It's the temple, not the prom.) Also remember that hairdressers and photographers will not be allowed inside the temple, so do not plan on their services in that respect.

5. The exchanging of wedding rings is not part of the marriage ceremony in the temple. The temple wedding ceremony is not like the secular or civil weddings you may have seen. Don't be disappointed when they won't allow you to recite your own vows and exchange rings during the ceremony. The exchanging of rings may be done in the sealing room following the ceremony (away from the temple altar). Rings cannot be exchanged anywhere else in the temple or even on the temple grounds. A couple may choose to have a ring ceremony as part of their reception or open house later in the day. Many couples opt to participate in a ring ceremony so that family members or friends who could not attend the temple may feel included in the day's activities.

I feel that in order to respect the fact that the marriage has already been performed inside the temple, a couple should *never* present a ring ceremony to their guests as though it were the actual wedding ceremony. I once witnessed a beautiful ring ceremony in which the bishop stood alone beforehand and explained to the guests that the wedding had already taken place and that the couple was only going to exchange rings since that is not part of the temple wedding ceremony. He also explained a little about temple ceremonies and the sealing power that is offered there. The bishop then sat down, and the bride and groom stood and exchanged rings and a kiss without the participation of an officiator or the rest of their wedding party (to avoid looking as though it were the marriage ceremony).

6. Remind your temple guests of appropriate dress standards in the temple. Sealing rooms in most temples are small, and only endowed family members and close friends who have current recommends should be invited to your ceremony. Sunday attire is appropriate for guests to wear. Clothing such as formal bridesmaid dresses and tuxedos are not permitted or appropriate for a temple sealing ceremony.

Most of these mistakes can be avoided by closely reading and abiding to the information packet that the temple staff will mail to you after you reserve your wedding date with them.

Works Cited

Asay, Carlos E. "The Temple Garment: An Outward Expression of an Inward Covenant," *Temples of the Church of Jesus Christ of Latter-day Saints,* 1999.

Benson, Ezra Taft. "What I Hope You Teach Your Children About the Temple," *Tambuli.* April–May 1986.

Brown, Matthew B. and Paul Thomas Smith. *Symbols in Stone: Symbolism on the Early Temples of the Restoration.* American Fork, Utah: Covenant Communications, 1997.

Brown, Victor L. "Questions About Temple Marriage," *New Era,* Feb. 1987.

Charles, John D. *Endowed from on High: Understanding the Symbols of the Endowment.* Springville, Utah: Horizon Publishers, 1999.

Gaskill, Alonzo. *The Lost Language of Symbolism: An Essential Guide for Recognizing and Interpreting Symbols of the Gospel.* Salt Lake City: Deseret Book, 2003

Gaskill, Alonzo. *The Savior and the Serpent: Unlocking the Doctrine of the Fall.* Salt Lake City: Deseret Book, 2005.

Kimball, Spencer W. "God Will Not Be Mocked," *Ensign,* Oct. 1974.

McConkie, Bruce R. *A New Witness for the Articles of Faith*. Salt Lake City: Deseret Book, 1985.

Nelson, Russell M. "The Atonement," *Ensign*, Nov. 1996.

Nelson, Russell M. "Personal Preparation for Temple Blessings," *Ensign*, May 2001.

Old Testament: Gospel Doctrine Teacher's Manual. The Church of Jesus Christ of Latter-day Saints. Salt Lake City: Intellectual Reserve, 1996, 2001.

Our Heritage: A Brief History of the Church of Jesus Christ of Latter-day Saints. The Church of Jesus Christ of Latter-day Saints. Salt Lake City: Intellectual Reserve, 1996.

Packer, Boyd K. *The Holy Temple*. Salt Lake City: Bookcraft, Inc., 1980.

Scott, Richard G. "Receive the Temple Blessings," *Ensign*, May 1999.

Smith, Joseph Fielding (comp.). *Teachings of the Prophet Joseph Smith: Collectors Edition*. American Fork, Utah: Covenant Communications, Inc., 2005.

Webb, Kimberly. "Exploring: The Nauvoo Temple," *Friend*, June 2002.

Widtsoe, John A. (comp.). *Discourses of Brigham Young*. Salt Lake City: Deseret Book, 1977.

Widtsoe, John A. "Temple Worship." *Utah Genealogical and Historical Magazine*, Apr. 1921.

Wilcox, S. Michael. *House of Glory: Finding Personal Meaning in the Temple*. Salt Lake City: Deseret Book, 1995.

About the *Author*

Brittany Mangus was born and raised in Utah. She graduated from West Jordan High School and Salt Lake Community College. She married her sweetheart, Que Mangus, in the Salt Lake Temple in 2001. They currently live in the Salt Lake valley with their golden retriever, Madison, and their cat, Parley P. Cat.

When she's not working, she enjoys reading about Joseph Smith and the temple, remodeling homes with Que (she designs, he builds), playing the piano, and reading books by her favorite authors, Jane Austen and Edith Wharton.